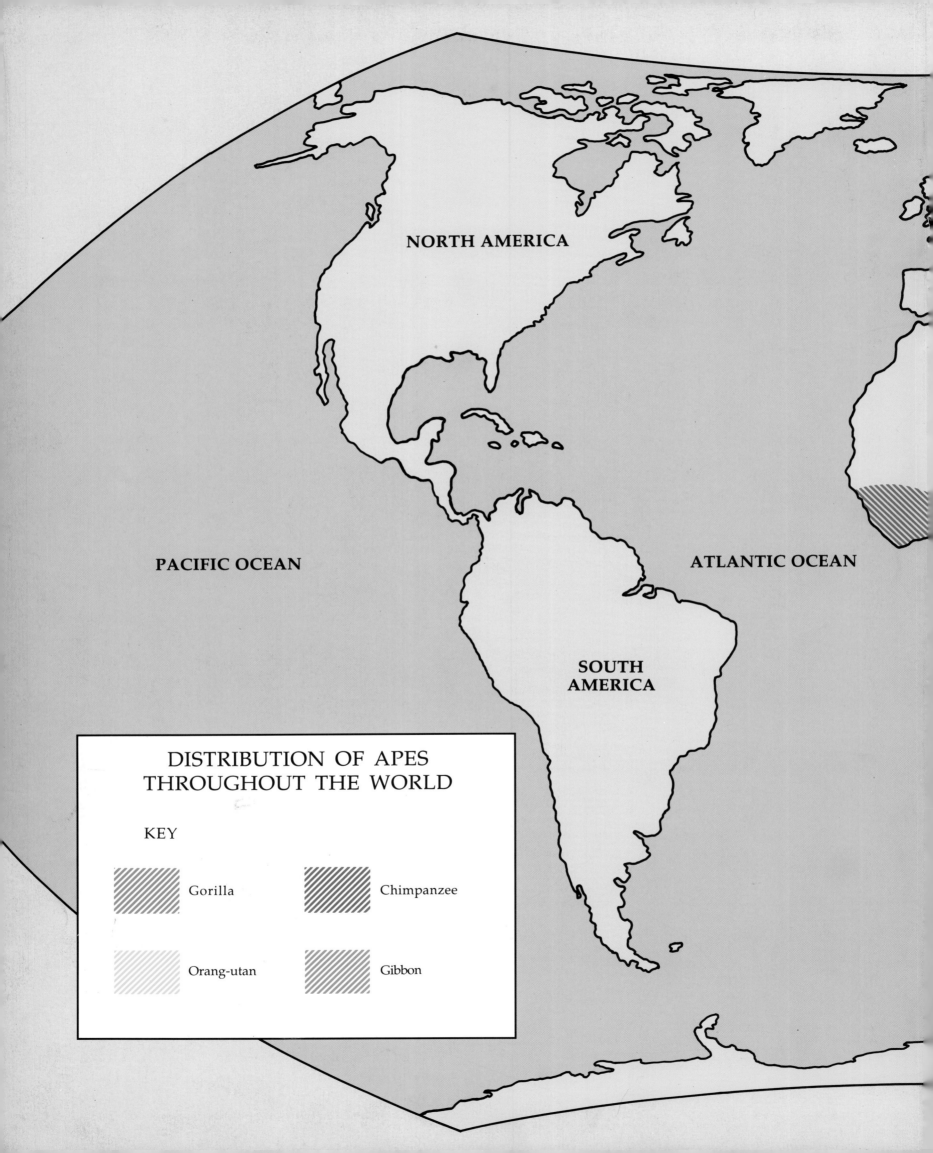

NORTH AMERICA

PACIFIC OCEAN

ATLANTIC OCEAN

SOUTH
AMERICA

DISTRIBUTION OF APES
THROUGHOUT THE WORLD

KEY

Gorilla

Chimpanzee

Orang-utan

Gibbon

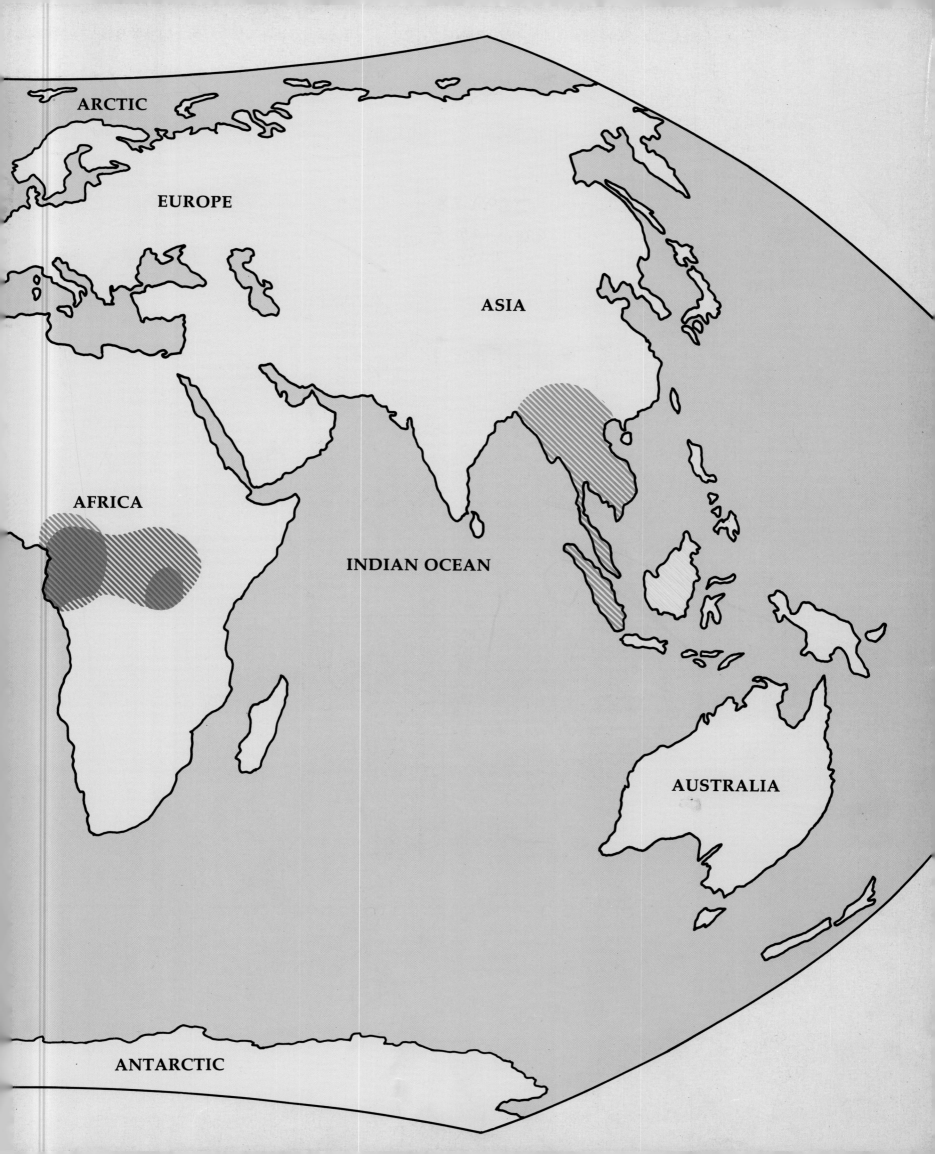

For Shirley and Cyril
T. L.

For Alain, the artiste
J. B.

First published in 1993 by
David Bennett Books Ltd
94 Victoria Street
St Albans
Herts, AL1 3TG

BRITISH LIBRARY CATALOGUING IN PUBLICATION DATA
A catalogue record for this book is available
from the British Library.
ISBN 1 85602 097 5

Editor: Karen Filsell
Designer: Roger Hands

Typesetting by Type City
Production by Imago
Printed in Singapore

The author of this book was someone who both loved monkeys and apes and
understood them. Tess Lemmon worked with woolly monkeys, at the Woolly Monkey
Sanctuary in Cornwall. She then went to the Gambia, in Africa, where she helped
look after orphaned chimpanzees, and for a year became mother to Polly, a baby
baboon, whom she successfully reintroduced back into baboon society. Tess was caring
and sensitive, but also brave enough to stand up for what she believed in. She
championed the cause of monkeys and apes, by her work for the International
Primate Protection League and support of organisations such as the Jane Goodall
Foundation, but also by using her skills as a writer to expose in print those who
continue to abuse primates.

APES

Written by
TESS LEMMON

Illustrated by
JOHN BUTLER

David Bennett Books

CONTENTS

gorilla
(*Gorilla gorilla*)

orang-utan
(*Pongo pygmaeus*)

male
Height: 170 cm
Weight: 140-180 kg

female
Height: 150 cm
Weight: 90 kg

male
Head & body: 97 cm
Weight: 60-90 kg

G ibbons

G orillas

C onservation

H ow to help apes

Although other apes are measured by the length of their head and body,
gorillas are always measured by their height when standing up.

chimpanzee
(*Pan troglodytes*)

gibbon (lar gibbon)
(*Hylobates lar*)

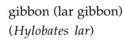

female
Head & body: 78 cm
Weight: 40-50 kg

male
Head & body: 77-92 cm
Weight: 40 kg

female
Head & body: 70-85 cm
Weight: 30 kg

male
Head & body: 45-65 cm
Weight: 5.7 kg

female
Head & body: 45-65 cm
Weight: 5.3 kg

Introduction

Gorillas, chimpanzees, orang-utans and gibbons are all apes. Apes, humans and monkeys are closely related, and belong to a group of animals called primates. Instead of hooves or paws, all primates have hands and feet that can hold and grasp. Gibbons are called lesser apes because they are smaller than the others, which are called great apes. Apes are all forest-dwellers, and they eat mainly fruit, leaves and insects.

The ancestor of all apes looked something like this.

Over millions of years, primates evolved from a mouselike creature that once lived in the trees.

The easiest way to tell an ape from a monkey is to remember that only monkeys have tails.

An ape's arms are longer than its legs. In trees, monkeys run along branches on all fours, but apes hold their bodies upright and swing their arms beneath the branches. This is why apes have such long, strong arms, and why they do not need tails to help them balance or grip.

On the ground, chimpanzees, gorillas and orang-utans use their strong arms to take their weight as they walk.

8

The hands and feet of an ape
resemble human hands. They have
a thumb separate from the four fingers,
and a big toe separate from the other
four toes. When they climb trees, they
can grasp branches with both their hands
and their feet.

*Apes rely on their
eyesight far more than
their sense of smell,
so their noses are small.*

*Orang-utans and chimpanzees
can hold fruit in their feet
as well as their hands.*

All apes are active during the day. Their eyes face forwards,
so they can see where they are going as they move through
the trees. They have excellent eyesight, and can see in colour,
whereas some animals see only in black and white. Colour
vision helps them tell when fruit is ready to eat: many
unripe fruits are green but, on ripening, turn yellow or red.

Some apes live in twos and threes, others live in groups of fifty or more. They spend their days looking for food, eating, resting and being with each other.

The great apes are too big to be killed and eaten by most animals. Sometimes a lion, leopard or snake snatches a youngster that has strayed from its mother, but this does not happen often. The lesser apes are hard to catch because they live so high in the trees.

Grooming one another is one way in which apes show affection. Two apes comb through each other's hair with their fingers to get rid of dry skin and dirt. This is so relaxing that sometimes the one being groomed falls asleep.

Apes usually have one baby at a time. The mother suckles and carries her baby for several years, so she could not manage more than one at a time.

Apes have a long childhood. Some are not grown up until they are fifteen years old. A young ape needs time to learn how to look after itself in the forest, and how to behave properly – such as being polite to its elders. It learns by watching its mother and others, and is told off for wrongdoings. Punishments include being screamed at or bitten.

thoughtful

frightened or excited

calling

Apes that live together get to know each other very well. They experience many different moods, including annoyance, curiosity and contentment. They express how they feel by the look on their faces, the way they move their bodies and the sounds they make – so it is very easy for one ape to tell the mood of another.

Every night, most apes make nests in the trees or on the ground. They bend and intertwine leafy branches, then pile more leaves and branches on top. The resulting springy mat is both comfortable and warm – for the forest can get rather chilly at night.

11

Orang-utans

Orang-utans are the world's largest tree-living mammals. They live in the hot jungles of Borneo and Sumatra, two islands in south-east Asia.

The people of Borneo and Sumatra have a legend that the orang-utan was once a man who did wrong, and fled to the jungle to escape being punished. Orang-utan means 'man of the woods'.

Orang-utans (or orangs) climb around very slowly and carefully because they are so heavy. They spread their weight across the branches by grasping them with their hands and feet. Their feet are so like hands that it is as if they have four hands. Even so, they sometimes make mistakes and come crashing down to the ground. Many orangs break their arms or legs in accidents, but these soon mend.

Too big to leap, orangs have found other ways of travelling from one tree to the next. Sometimes one can stretch across with its long arms, or else it rocks the tree it is in until the tree bends over and makes a bridge. If this is unsuccessful, the orang comes to the ground.

An orang walks on all fours, either on the palms of its hands or on its fists. Big males travel on the ground more often than females and youngsters, because the trees cannot always bear their weight.

During the monsoon season in Borneo and Sumatra, rain pours down in torrents for several hours every day, and the orang-utans get soaked to the skin. They do not like getting wet, and try to take shelter under leaves. Sometimes an orang breaks off a huge leaf to use as an umbrella.

The orang's long, shaggy hair comes in handy when it is thirsty. It dips its arm into the puddles that collect in tree holes, and sucks the drips from its hair.

13

Unlike all the other apes, orang-utans spend most of their time alone. Because of their size, they need to eat a great deal of food every day to stay alive. If lots of them lived together in the same area of the jungle, the food supplies would soon become exhausted.

Young orangs enjoy playing games.

Males and females come together to mate, but then the male goes away again. A female has her first baby when she is between seven and ten years old, and is not ready to mate again for about three years.

The female looks after the baby entirely on her own. For the first year of its life, the baby clings to her chest or back constantly, but after that it follows her around. By this time, it is eating solid food, but it continues to be suckled for about three years. When it is about four years old, its mother may have another baby, but the older child does not leave her until it is adult, at about seven years old.

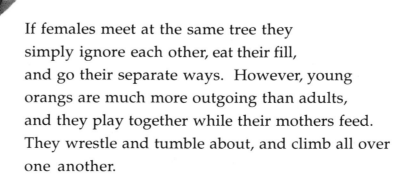

If females meet at the same tree they simply ignore each other, eat their fill, and go their separate ways. However, young orangs are much more outgoing than adults, and they play together while their mothers feed. They wrestle and tumble about, and climb all over one another.

Male orang-utans avoid one another by calling to announce their presence. When one male hears another, he goes in the opposite direction. Males call mostly when they get up in the morning and just before they go to sleep. The sound starts as a grumble and builds up to a roar that can be heard 2 km away – which is why it is called the 'long call'.

Bees, honey, ants and leaves all feature on an orang's menu – but mostly it eats fruit such as mangoes, durians and lychees. In the rain forest, different trees bear fruit at different times of the year, so orangs need to know where and when to look for food. Fortunately, they can remember not only where a particular tree is, but also when its fruit ripens.

The males of Sumatra have smaller cheek flaps than the males of Borneo.

The face of an adult male orang-utan looks nothing like a baby orang's face. The baby's face is quite human-like. The male has a beard and flaps of skin on each side of his face.

Sumatran male orang-utan

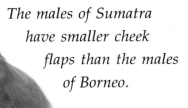

Bornean males have darker hair, rounder heads and short moustaches.

Each male has a pouch of skin at his throat, which he fills with air to make his voice even louder. The pouch looks like an enormous double chin when it is empty.

Bornean male orang-utan

15

Chimpanzees

Chimpanzees live in the forests of eastern, western and central Africa. Some of these forests are thick, tangled tropical rain forests. Others are open woodlands, with patches of grassland. Chimpanzees generally travel on the ground, but climb trees to find fruit and leaves to eat, or to chase prey.

Big ears help chimpanzees to hear well. When they are out of sight in the forest they hoot to keep in contact.

Up to 120 chimpanzees live together in a community. Any one part of the forest does not usually provide enough food for all of them, so the chimps divide into smaller groups to feed. Males often team up together, and females go with their offspring. Sometimes the whole community will assemble to feast on a tree laden with fruit.

Once, humans were thought to be the only animals clever enough to use tools, but now we know that chimpanzees use tools such as sticks or stones, too. A stone to crack open a nut is chosen carefully. It has to be heavy enough to break the shell, but not so heavy that it squashes the kernel.

On the ground, chimpanzees walk on all fours. This is called knuckle-walking, because they put the backs of their fingers against the ground.

Chimpanzees regularly eat insects, monkeys and antelope. Monkeys are hard to catch because they escape through the trees, so five or six chimps may hunt them together. They surround a troop of monkeys, then some of the group will pick out a single monkey and chase it towards the others, who are waiting to catch it. Sometimes the monkeys scream at the chimps and chase them away.

Chimpanzees live for forty or fifty years.

Elderly chimps sometimes go grey and bald.

Deep in the forests of Zaïre, in central Africa, lives an animal so closely related to chimpanzees that, when it was first discovered, it was called the pygmy chimpanzee. It is now named the bonobo, after a town in Zaïre.

The bonobo is much the same size as the chimpanzee. However, it is more graceful and lightly built. The bonobo has smaller ears than the chimpanzee, a central parting and long sideburns. A bonobo's life is very similar to that of a chimpanzee.

17

All the chimpanzees in one community know one another very well. Mothers have a very strong bond with their children, and many non-related chimps form close friendships. Some individuals are more important than others. These dominant ones help themselves to the best food, and the other chimps show them respect, by crouching in front of them when they meet. Adult males are dominant over females – and most arguments flare up when young adult males try to take over from older ones. Most males stay in the same community all their lives, but grown-up females leave home and join another community.

Each community lives in one area of forest, and groups of males patrol the boundaries of their territory. If they meet chimps from neighbouring communities, they try to scare them away by standing up to make themselves look bigger and by making their hair stand on end. Then they charge around screaming and throwing branches. If this does not work, fights break out.

Hugging, kissing and back-patting are all ways in which chimpanzees show their affection for one another. Grooming one another is a particularly important expression of friendship.

18

A female chimpanzee has her first baby when she is about thirteen years old. For the first few months, the baby clings to her hairy chest, but as it becomes heavier, it rides around on her back. The mother will not have another baby until the first one starts to look after itself, at about five years old. Even when they have become adults, between thirteen and fifteen years old, chimpanzees spend a lot of time with their mothers.

A young chimp suckles from its mother for five years, but begins to eat solid food between three and five months old. Sometimes its mother gives it food, but usually it picks up any scraps she drops, or chews the other end of whatever she is eating. It also begs for food by putting its mouth up to hers, and she lets it take pieces out of her mouth.

Playing is important, because it helps chimpanzees get to know each other, and teaches them to control their own strength. Young chimps wrestle, chase and play tug-of-war with sticks. They usually play with their elder brothers and sisters and their mothers.

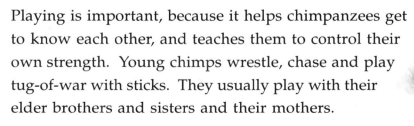

Gibbons

Gibbons are the smallest apes. They live in the tropical forests of south-east Asia, in countries such as Thailand and Malaysia. Since these forests are cut off from each other by seas and rivers, species of gibbon differ greatly from forest to forest.

The pileated gibbon has pale tufts of hair at the side of its head.

The siamang is bigger than any of the others, and almost twice as heavy.

The concolor gibbon has a more pointed head than the others.

Some gibbons are pale yellow, some are jet black, some are silvery grey – and some even change colour during their lifetimes! They are born a light colour, turn darker, then become light again. In some species, males and females are different colours. For example, the female hoolock gibbon is golden, and the male is black.

Gibbons are the acrobats of the ape world. They use their long arms to hang from high branches and swing along at top speed – and when they leap across gaps, it looks as if they are flying. They swing by holding on, first with one arm, then the other, and their long fingers hook over the branches.

Gibbons cannot walk on all fours because their arms are so much longer than their legs. Instead, they walk upright and hold their arms above their heads to keep them out of the way. Gibbons hardly ever come to the ground, but, when they stand up in the trees, they look like tightrope walkers.

Gibbons are the only apes that do not build nests. They sleep sitting up in the forks of branches. They are quite comfortable because they have pads of skin on their backsides, which are like built-in cushions.

Gibbons are the only apes to live in pairs, and mate for life. A male and female often have two or three children of different ages living with them. The whole family travels through the trees every day in search of ripe fruit, leaves and shoots to eat. Being so small and light, gibbons can hang from the tips of branches and reach fruit growing right at the ends.

Gibbons are the most territorial of the apes. If one male wants to take over another's territory, they usually manage to settle the dispute without fighting. They try to scare each other by shaking branches and leaping about. Sometimes, two enemies sit face to face in neighbouring trees and sing at each other, until one gives up and goes away.

Well-hidden in the leafy treetops, gibbons are more likely to be heard than seen – for the first thing they do, when they wake up in the morning, is sing. The male starts hooting and whooping, then the female joins in. Their duet lasts at least fifteen minutes. The noise carries far and wide. When other gibbons hear it, they know they must avoid that part of the forest because it is another family's home.

The siamang has a throat pouch of loose skin that expands with air to the size of its head, when it sings. This makes its voice even louder. Some other gibbons have these pouches too, but not such big ones.

Female gibbons have a baby every two or three years. Some father apes do not take much interest in their children, but gibbon fathers groom their children and play with them. When a siamang baby is about eight months old, its father carries it during the day, and hands it back to its mother at night.

When they are grown up, at eight years old, gibbons leave their parents to find a mate and live in their own patch of forest. They break away gradually, spending more and more time by themselves. Their parents become more hostile towards them, and sometimes scream to make them go away.

Gorillas

mountain gorilla

Gorillas are the largest apes. They live mostly on the ground because they are too big to live in the trees. There are three races of gorilla, and they live in different parts of central Africa.

The western lowland gorilla lives in Cameroon, the Central African Republic, Gabon, Congo, Equatorial Guinea and Nigeria. The eastern lowland gorilla lives only in eastern Zaïre, and the mountain gorilla lives in Rwanda, Uganda and Zaïre. The two races never meet because the mountain gorilla lives between 1,700-3,800 m up the mountains. The mountain gorilla has longer hair to keep it warm in the cold climate.

eastern lowland gorilla

All gorillas live in forests with clearings where the light reaches the ground and encourages plants to grow. Gorillas eat these plants, so they have no trouble finding food. They sit in a clearing and help themselves to huge bunches. Like humans, they eat certain parts of different plants: sometimes only the leaves or the stalk or the root. Wild celery, wild ginger and nettles are some of their favourites. Between meals, gorillas snooze and sunbathe. Resting helps them digest their food.

Plants need a great deal of chewing, so the gorilla has big teeth. It also has very strong jaws, worked by muscles running all the way from the top of its head. This is why gorillas have big heads.

eastern lowland gorilla

In order to provide themselves with enough energy, gorillas eat enormous meals that last 2 or 3 hours at a time. They start with a big breakfast, have snacks during the day, and another meal before going to sleep. An adult male munches through 20-30 kg of greens every day. Gorillas also eat insects and fruit.

Even though gorillas are so big, they are difficult to see when they sit in the undergrowth. You could walk right past them without knowing they were there. Sometimes their voices give them away. While they eat, they smack their lips and grunt with enjoyment.

Gorillas live in groups of about twelve animals. Each group is made up of several adult females and their young, plus one adult male.

The biggest adult male is the leader of the group. When he starts walking, everyone else follows him. When he sits down, the others sit too. He is called a silverback, because the hair on his back is a silver colour. Young males whose hair has not yet changed colour are called blackbacks.

The silverback is very big and strong, but also very gentle. Young gorillas play with him by jumping on his head or pulling his hair, but he does not mind at all. If he gets tired of it he just stares at them, and that is enough to make them stop.

New-born gorillas are only about half the size of a new-born human baby. Snuggled in its mother's hair, a baby gorilla can hardly be seen.

When it is about two months old, a baby gorilla starts to crawl. At eight to nine months old it can walk, but it continues taking rides on its mother's back until it is three or four years old. Gorillas stay close to their mothers until they are grown up, at about ten years old. Most adult gorillas leave the group to find mates and start groups of their own.

A gorilla group keeps together all the time, whether resting, travelling or eating. Anyone who gets out of sight makes little grunting sounds to let the others know where he or she is.

When they play with each other, young gorillas get so excited that they stand upright and beat their chests. Adults beat their chests when they are angry or worried – for example, when they hear an odd sound, or suddenly come upon a buffalo or an elephant. The silverback beats his chest when he meets other gorillas, as a warning to tell the strangers to go away. Gorillas hardly ever fight. They want to be left in peace with their own group.

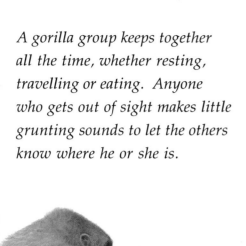

Conservation

For thousands of years, apes have been living in peace in the forests where they belong. But now that peace has been broken by humans, who kill or capture them and destroy their homes. Because of humans, apes are in danger of dying out completely.

The biggest threat to all apes is the destruction of their habitat, without which they cannot survive. People have always cut down trees to make space for themselves. Now there are more and more people in the world, needing more and more space. Time and again, thick forests are being replaced by houses or fields for food crops.

If forests were destroyed only to make way for local people, there might still be enough left for the apes. But many trees are cut down to provide wood for people in faraway countries, such as the USA, Japan and Britain. The trees are turned into products such as doors, saucepan handles and toilet seats. These things could easily be made from other kinds of wood, or from other materials.

Chimpanzees

Baby chimps are kept as pets in Africa and abroad. They are also smuggled into Spain, where they are dressed up and used by photographers, who take pictures of people holding them. They are drugged to keep them quiet, and wearing clothes makes their hair fall out. Most of them die within a few months.

Gibbons

Baby gibbons are kept in tiny cages in local markets and sold as pets. Many die from starvation and neglect. Some gibbons (and chimpanzees) are sold to scientists abroad, who carry out experiments on them. Apes are so like humans that they are used to test drugs and medicines, for example.

Gorillas

The mountain gorilla is one of the most endangered animals in the world. There are only a few hundred of them left. Hunters used to kill gorillas and sell their hands and heads as souvenirs. They are now protected by armed guards who patrol the forests. Nowadays, hunters trespass into the forests to set snares for antelope, which they eat. Sadly, gorillas can get caught in these snares. Lowland gorillas are still in demand by some zoos.

Orang-utans

There are more orang-utans living in parts of the modern city of Taipei, in Taiwan, than in some parts of the jungles where they belong. There is a craze in Taipei for keeping them as pets, but they are often abandoned, and found wandering around shopping centres. Orangs are also kept as pets or performing animals in other countries, including the USA.

How to help apes

Although apes are in danger, people from all over the world are working to save and look after them. Some of the organisations are listed below – why not write and see how you can help? Make sure you include a stamped, addressed envelope when you write to them.

The International Primate Protection League (IPPL)

When she saw baby monkeys stacked up in crates at an airport, Dr Shirley McGreal decided to set up IPPL to help all primates. IPPL tracks down illegal animal dealers and runs a sanctuary for ex-laboratory gibbons. It also supports Chimfunshi Wildlife Orphanage in Zambia, Africa, which looks after rescued chimps.

Mr C Rosen, International Primate Protection League,
116 Judd Street, London, WC1H 9NS

The Dian Fossey Gorilla Fund

Sadly, there are only 600 mountain gorillas left in the world. They live in leafy forests high in the Virunga Volcanoes in central Africa. When Dian Fossey's favourite gorilla, Digit, was speared to death by poachers, she set up a fund to help protect the last remaining mountain gorillas.

The Dian Fossey Gorilla Fund,
110 Gloucester Avenue,
London, NW1 8JA

The Jane Goodall Institute

Jane Goodall has been studying chimps for 30 years, and is the world expert on them. She set up her Institute to help all chimps everywhere, including those in captivity and in medical research. The Institute has a Chimpanzee Guardian Scheme for adopting orphan chimps being looked after in its sanctuaries in Uganda, Congo and Burundi. It is also planning a sanctuary in Glasgow for chimps illegally exported to Europe for the entertainment trade, and for those being retired from medical research.

Dilys Vass, The Jane Goodall Institute (UK),
15 Clarendon Park,
Lymington,
Hants, SO41 8AX

The Orang-utan Foundation

This Foundation was set up by Dr Birute Galdikas, who has been studying orang-utans for many years. She also rescues ex-pets and teaches them how to live in the jungle again.

Ashley Leiman, The Orang-utan Foundation,
7 Kent Terrace, London NW1 4RP